LOOPS & SORTING

by Teddy Borth

Cody Koala
An Imprint of Pop!
popbooksonline.com

abdobooks.com

Published by Pop!, a division of ABDO, PO Box 398166, Minneapolis, Minnesota 55439. Copyright © 2022 by Abdo Consulting Group, Inc. International copyrights reserved in all countries. No part of this book may be reproduced in any form without written permission from the publisher. Cody Koala™ is a trademark and logo of Pop!.

Printed in China
052021
092021
THIS BOOK CONTAINS RECYCLED MATERIALS

Cover Photo: Shutterstock Images
Interior Photos: iStockphotos, 7, 15 (top), 15 (bottom center), 19, 21; Shutterstock Images, 9, 10, 13 (top), 13 (bottom center), 13, (bottom left), 13 (bottom right), 15 (bottom left), 16

Editor: Elizabeth Andrews
Series Designer: Laura Graphenteen

Library of Congress Control Number: 2020948281
Publisher's Cataloging-in-Publication Data
Names: Borth, Teddy, author.
Title: Loops & sorting / by Teddy Borth
Description: Minneapolis, Minnesota : Pop!, 2022 | Series: Coding basics | Includes online resources and index.
Identifiers: ISBN 9781532169656 (lib. bdg.) | ISBN 9781098240585 (ebook)
Subjects: LCSH: Loops (Computer science)--Juvenile literature. | Sorting (Electronic computers)--Juvenile literature. | Computer programming--Juvenile literature.
Classification: DDC 005.1--dc23

Hello! My name is

Cody Koala

Pop open this book and you'll find QR codes like this one, loaded with information, so you can learn even more!

Scan this code* and others like it while you read, or visit the website below to make this book pop.

popbooksonline.com/loops-sort

*Scanning QR codes requires a web-enabled smart device with a QR code reader app and a camera.

Table of Contents

Chapter 1
Again and Again 4

Chapter 2
Life Loops 8

Chapter 3
Putting It in Order 14

Chapter 4
Run It Again! 20

Making Connections 22
Glossary 23
Index 24
Online Resources 24

Chapter 1

Again and Again

Loops are blocks of **code** that get repeated until the job is done. **Coders** use loops to make the code shorter.

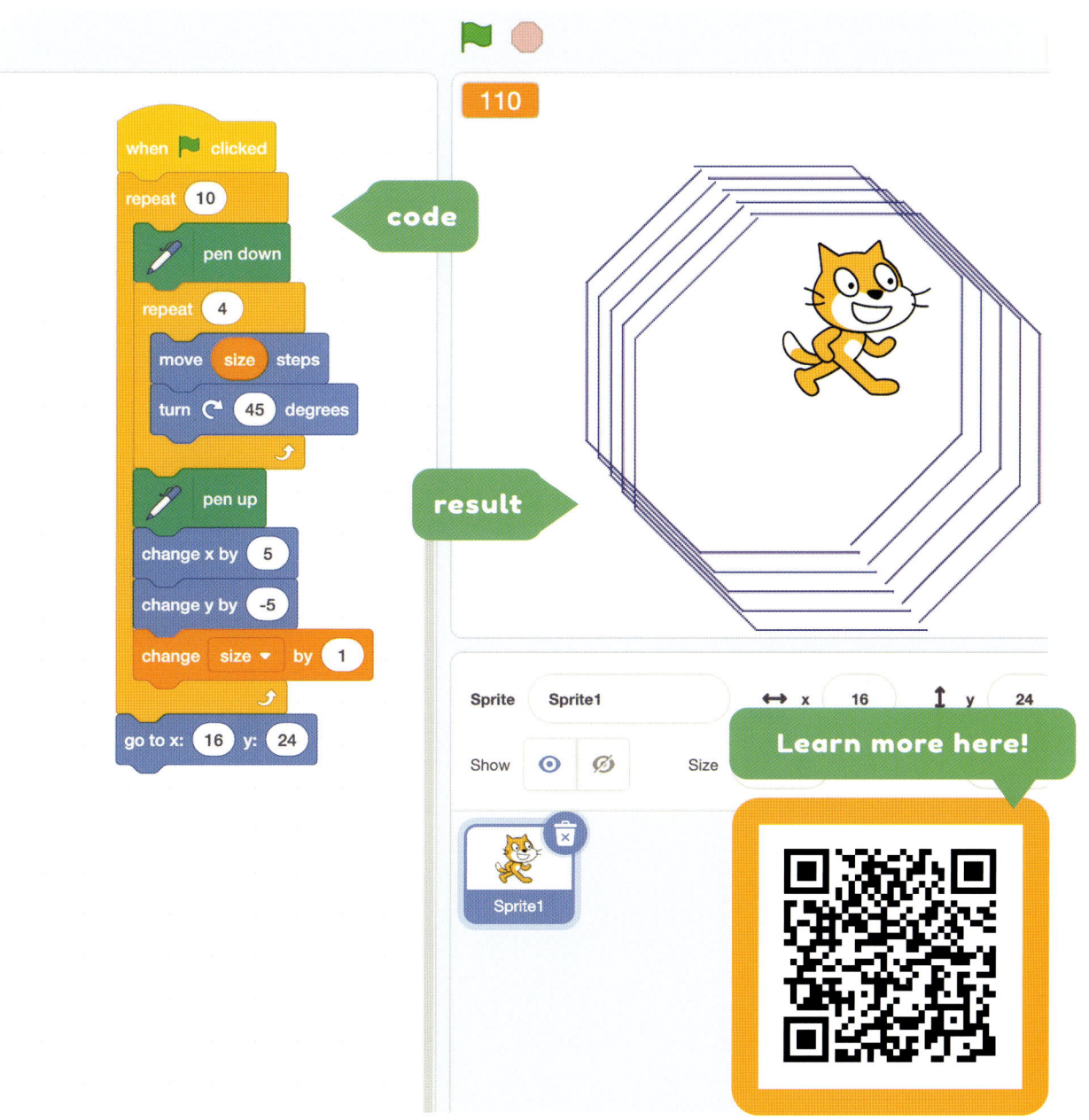

Loops are great for any **repetitive** tasks. The school bus runs on a loop. Every morning it drives the same roads. It makes the same stops. Mia's bus stop is after the park. She knows she will be next!

Chapter 2

Life Loops

School is on a loop. It starts and ends at the same times. Classes have an order. Jack has math class now. After math he gets to go to lunch! His stomach reminds him at this time every day.

board game

Erin plays a game with her friends. Everybody takes turns playing until the game ends. It is on a loop!

> The rules of the game are instructions. Players follow the rules, like a computer would follow code!

Dan eats a salad. Eating is like being in a loop. Put the food on the fork. Bring the food to the mouth. Chew. Swallow. Repeat until full!

> The largest salad on record was in Russia and weighed over 44,000 pounds (20,100 kg). That would take a lot of loops to eat!

0000111001000100111001001001100101000

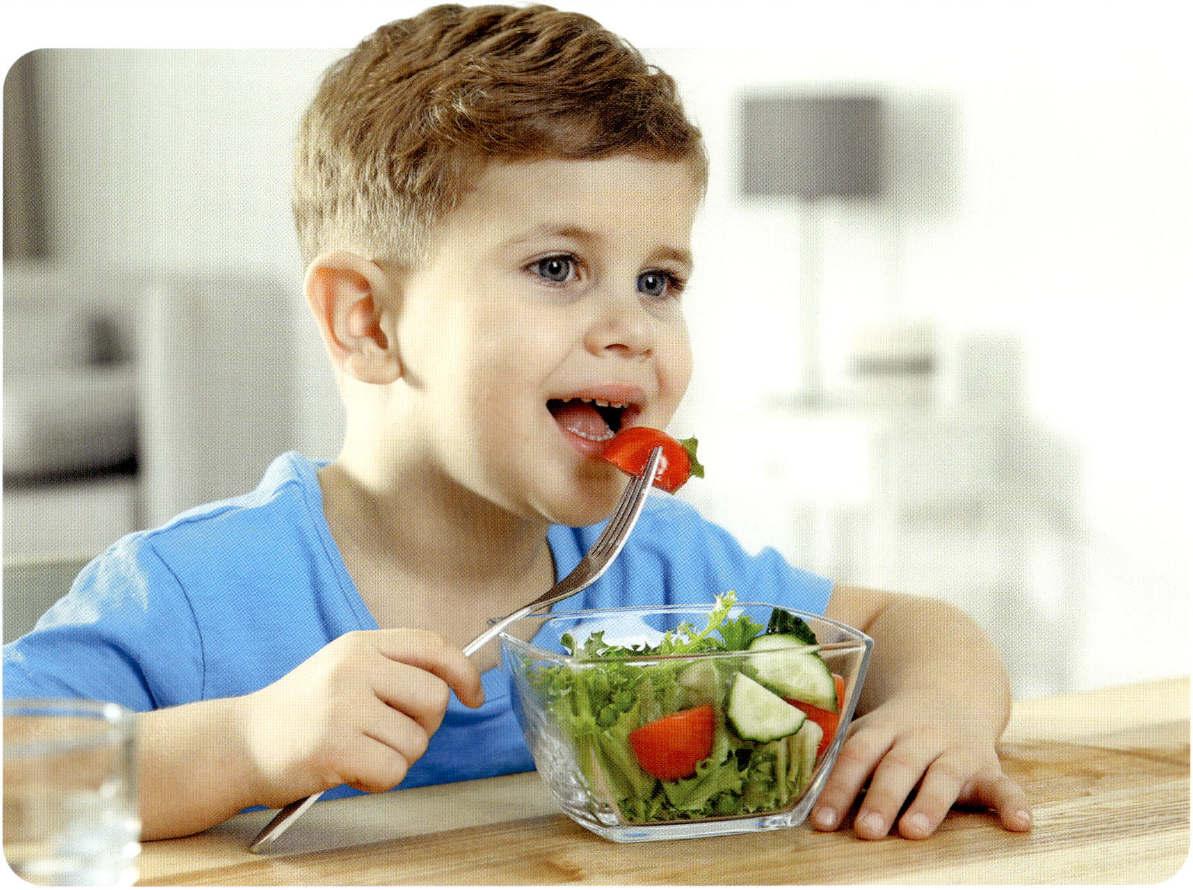

1000111001000100111001001001100110010

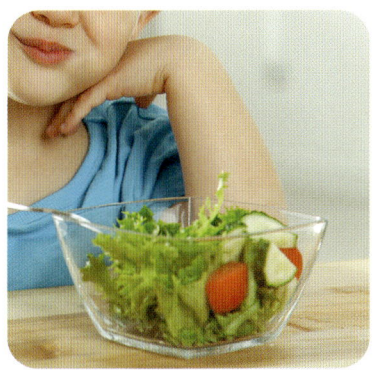

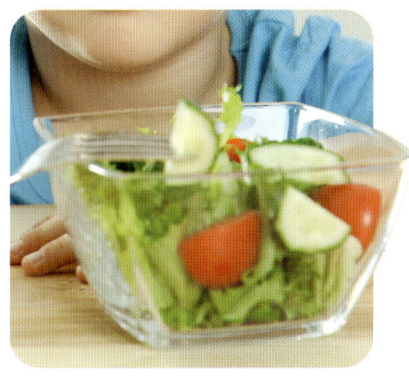

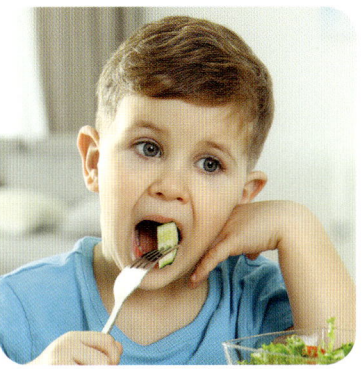

Chapter 3

Putting It in Order

Loops are important for sorting. Sorting puts things in order. It takes a lot of work for computers to sort things. They can only **compare** two things at a time. A smarter loop will make sorting faster.

yellow bin

red bin

blue bin

Watch a Video Here!

Beth sorts her bookshelf. She uses a loop. She compares the first book to the second book. The first book should be after the second. She swaps the books. She repeats this over and over as she compares each book.

Nate wants to sort his toys by size. Nate has an idea to make his sorting easier. He first puts his toys into groups. He puts all the small toys in one pile. He puts large toys in a different pile. He then sorts each pile.

Chapter 4

Run It Again!

Sorting takes many steps. The more items you have, the more times you loop. What things do you do over and over? You use loops every day, just like **coders**!

Learn more here!

Making Connections

Text-to-Self

Your school schedule runs in a loop. What do you do first at school each day? What is next?

Text-to-Text

Have you read other books about loops or sorting? What did you learn?

Text-to-World

Stores usually sort their products into groups. Toys are all in one section. Shoes are in another section. What else is sorted in a group at a store?

Glossary

code – a list of instructions that tells a computer what to do.

coder – a person who builds programs or works with computer languages.

compare – to look at two or more things and note what is the same and what is different between them.

repetitive – involving doing the same thing or happening in the same way several times.

Index

book, 17

code, 4, 11, 20

computer, 11, 14

loop, 4, 8, 11, 12, 14, 17, 20

school, 7, 8

toy, 11, 18

Online Resources

popbooksonline.com

Thanks for reading this Cody Koala book!

Scan this code* and others like it in this book, or visit the website below to make this book pop!

popbooksonline.com/loops-sort

*Scanning QR codes requires a web-enabled smart device with a QR code reader app and a camera.